The

Ideal Church Record

(FOR INTERDENOMINATIONAL USE)

A Permanent Record

for

Churches

with

Membership Record Arranged Alphabetically

Published by

BETHEL PUBLISHING COMPANY

1819 S. Main St.

Elkhart, IN 46516

Index

ISBN 0-934998-01-9

Record of

Name of Church____

Name of Denomination____

Location of Church____

Date of Organization
of Local Church____

Date of Arrangement
of Permanent Record____

P A S T O R S

NAME	Date of Ordination	DATE OF SERVICE		REMARKS
		Began	Ended	

P A S T O R S

NAME	Date of Ordination	DATE OF SERVICE		REMARKS
		Began	Ended	

O F F I C E R S

Deacon, Class Leader, Treasurer, Steward, S.S. Superintendent, Official Board Member or Other Officer

NAME	Date of Election	DATE OF SERVICE		OFFICE HELD
		Began	Ended	

OFFICERS

Deacon, Class Leader, Treasurer, Steward, S.S. Superintendent, Official Board Member or Other Officer

NAME	Date of Election	DATE OF SERVICE		OFFICE HELD
		Began	Ended	

OFFICERS

Deacon, Class Leader, Treasurer, Steward, S.S. Superintendent, Official Board Member or Other Officer

NAME	Date of Election	DATE OF SERVICE		OFFICE HELD
		Began	Ended	

OFFICERS

Deacon, Class Leader, Treasurer, Steward, S.S. Superintendent, Official Board Member or Other Officer

NAME	Date of Election	DATE OF SERVICE		OFFICE HELD
		Began	Ended	

OFFICERS

Deacon, Class Leader, Treasurer, Steward, S.S. Superintendent, Official Board Member or Other Officer

NAME	Date of Election	DATE OF SERVICE Began	Ended	OFFICE HELD

OFFICERS

Deacon, Class Leader, Treasurer, Steward, S.S. Superintendent, Official Board Member or Other Officer

NAME	Date of Election	DATE OF SERVICE Began	Ended	OFFICE HELD

OFFICERS

Deacon, Class Leader, Treasurer, Steward, S.S. Superintendent, Official Board Member or Other Officer

NAME	Date of Election	DATE OF SERVICE		OFFICE HELD
		Began	Ended	

OFFICERS

Deacon, Class Leader, Treasurer, Steward, S.S. Superintendent, Official Board Member or Other Officer

NAME	Date of Election	DATE OF SERVICE		OFFICE HELD
		Began	Ended	

OFFICERS

Deacon, Class Leader, Treasurer, Steward, S.S. Superintendent, Official Board Member or Other Officer

NAME	Date of Election	DATE OF SERVICE		OFFICE HELD
		Began	Ended	

OFFICERS

Deacon, Class Leader, Treasurer, Steward, S.S. Superintendent, Official Board Member or Other Officer

NAME	Date of Election	DATE OF SERVICE Began	DATE OF SERVICE Ended	OFFICE HELD

OFFICERS

Deacon, Class Leader, Treasurer, Steward, S.S. Superintendent, Official Board Member or Other Officer

NAME	Date of Election	DATE OF SERVICE		OFFICE HELD
		Began	Ended	

OFFICERS

Deacon, Class Leader, Treasurer, Steward, S.S. Superintendent, Official Board Member or Other Officer

NAME	Date of Election	DATE OF SERVICE		OFFICE HELD
		Began	Ended	

RECORD OF MEMBERSHIP

Check Those No Longer Members	NAME	Date of Birth	RESIDENCE	RECEIVED			
				HOW			WHEN
				Confes-sion	Transfer	Letter	

NOTE—By "Transfer" is meant the change of membership, by proper authority, from one loc

RECORD OF MEMBERSHIP

RECEIVED			REMOVED						REMARKS
BY WHOM	Date of Baptism	Date of Dedication by Parents	Transfer	Letter	Expelled	Withdrawn	Died	WHEN	(Where received, removed to what page, also what name if a woman and married since making of Record, cause of removal if expelled or withdrawn, etc.)

urch to another of the same denomination; by "Letter," from one denomination to another.

RECORD OF MEMBERSHIP

Check Those No Longer Members	NAME	Date of Birth	RESIDENCE	RECEIVED			
				HOW			WHEN
				Confes-sion	Transfer	Letter	

NOTE—By "Transfer" is meant the change of membership, by proper authority, from one loc

RECORD OF MEMBERSHIP

RECEIVED BY WHOM	Date of Baptism	Date of Dedication by Parents	REMOVED Transfer	Letter	Expelled	Withdrawn	Died	WHEN	REMARKS (Where received, removed to what page, also what name if a woman and married since making of Record, cause of removal if expelled or withdrawn, etc.)

rch to another of the same denomination; by "Letter," from one denomination to another.

RECORD OF MEMBERSHIP

Check Those No Longer Members	NAME	Date of Birth	RESIDENCE	RECEIVED			
				HOW			WHEN
				Confes-sion	Transfer	Letter	

NOTE—By "Transfer" is meant the change of membership, by proper authority, from one loc

RECORD OF MEMBERSHIP

RECEIVED	Date of Baptism	Date of Dedication by Parents	REMOVED						REMARKS (Where received, removed to what page, also what name if a woman and married since making of Record, cause of removal if expelled or withdrawn, etc.)
BY WHOM			Transfer	Letter	Expelled	Withdrawn	Died	WHEN	

rch to another of the same denomination; by "Letter," from one denomination to another.

RECORD OF MEMBERSHIP

Check Those No Longer Members	NAME	Date of Birth	RESIDENCE	RECEIVED			
				HOW			WHEN
				Confes-sion	Transfer	Letter	

NOTE—By "Transfer" is meant the change of membership, by proper authority, from one loca

RECORD OF MEMBERSHIP

RECEIVED BY WHOM	Date of Baptism	Date of Dedication by Parents	REMOVED Transfer	Letter	Expelled	Withdrawn	Died	WHEN	REMARKS (Where received, removed to what page, also what name if a woman and married since making of Record, cause of removal if expelled or withdrawn, etc.)

church to another of the same denomination; by "Letter," from one denomination to another.

RECORD OF MEMBERSHIP

Check Those No Longer Members	NAME	Date of Birth	RESIDENCE	RECEIVED — HOW: Confes-sion	RECEIVED — HOW: Transfer	RECEIVED — HOW: Letter	RECEIVED — WHEN

NOTE—By "Transfer" is meant the change of membership, by proper authority, from one local

RECORD OF MEMBERSHIP

RECEIVED BY WHOM	Date of Baptism	Date of Dedication by Parents	REMOVED Transfer	Letter	Expelled	Withdrawn	Died	WHEN	REMARKS (Where received, removed to what page, also what name if a woman and married since making of Record, cause of removal if expelled or withdrawn, etc.)

church to another of the same denomination; by "Letter," from one denomination to another.

RECORD OF MEMBERSHIP

Check Those No Longer Members	NAME	Date of Birth	RESIDENCE	RECEIVED			
				HOW			WHEN
				Confes-sion	Transfer	Letter	

NOTE—By "Transfer" is meant the change of membership, by proper authority, from one local

RECORD OF MEMBERSHIP

RECEIVED BY WHOM	Date of Baptism	Date of Dedication by Parents	REMOVEL* Transfer	Letter	Expelled	Withdrawn	Died	WHEN	REMARKS (Where received, removed to what page, also what name if a woman and married since making of Record, cause of removal if expelled or withdrawn, etc.)

church to another of the same denomination; by "Letter," from one denomination to another.

RECORD OF MEMBERSHIP

Check Those No Longer Members	NAME	Date of Birth	RESIDENCE	RECEIVED			
				HOW			WHEN
				Confes-sion	Transfer	Letter	

NOTE—By "Transfer" is meant the change of membership, by proper authority, from one local

RECORD OF MEMBERSHIP

RECEIVED BY WHOM	Date of Baptism	Date of Dedication by Parents	REMOVED Transfer	Letter	Expelled	Withdrawn	Died	WHEN	REMARKS (Where received, removed to what page, also what name if a woman and married since making of Record, cause of removal if expelled or withdrawn, etc.)

hurch to another of the same denomination; by "Letter," from one denomination to another.

RECORD OF MEMBERSHIP

Check Those No Longer Members	NAME	Date of Birth	RESIDENCE	RECEIVED			
				HOW			WHEN
				Confes-sion	Transfer	Letter	

NOTE—By "Transfer" is meant the change of membership, by proper authority, from one loca

RECORD OF MEMBERSHIP

RECEIVED BY WHOM	Date of Baptism	Date of Dedication by Parents	REMOVED Transfer	Letter	Expelled	Withdrawn	Died	WHEN	REMARKS (Where received, removed to what page, also what name if a woman and married since making of Record, cause of removal if expelled or withdrawn, etc.)

rch to another of the same denomination; by "Letter," from one denomination to another.

RECORD OF MEMBERSHIP

Check Those No Longer Members	NAME	Date of Birth	RESIDENCE	RECEIVED			
				HOW			WHEN
				Confes-sion	Transfer	Letter	

NOTE—By "Transfer" is meant the change of membership, by proper authority, from one loc

RECORD OF MEMBERSHIP

RECEIVED BY WHOM	Date of Baptism	Date of Dedication by Parents	REMOVED Transfer	Letter	Expelled	Withdrawn	Died	WHEN	REMARKS (Where received, removed to what page, also what name if a woman and married since making of Record, cause of removal if expelled or withdrawn, etc.)

rch to another of the same denomination; by "Letter," from one denomination to another.

RECORD OF MEMBERSHIP

Check Those No Longer Members	NAME	Date of Birth	RESIDENCE	RECEIVED			
				HOW			WHEN
				Confes-sion	Transfer	Letter	

NOTE—By "Transfer" is meant the change of membership, by proper authority, from one loc

RECORD OF MEMBERSHIP

RECEIVED BY WHOM	Date of Baptism	Date of Dedication by Parents	REMOVED Transfer	Letter	Expelled	Withdrawn	Died	WHEN	REMARKS (Where received, removed to what page, also what name if a woman and married since making of Record, cause of removal if expelled or withdrawn, etc.)

rch to another of the same denomination; by "Letter," from one denomination to another.

RECORD OF MEMBERSHIP

Check Those No Longer Members	NAME	Date of Birth	RESIDENCE	RECEIVED			
				HOW			WHEN
				Confes-sion	Transfer	Letter	

NOTE—By "Transfer" is meant the change of membership, by proper authority, from one loca

RECORD OF MEMBERSHIP

RECEIVED BY WHOM	Date of Baptism	Date of Dedication by Parents	REMOVED Transfer	Letter	Expelled	Withdrawn	Died	WHEN	REMARKS (Where received, removed to what page, also what name if a woman and married since making of Record, cause of removal if expelled or withdrawn, etc.)

rch to another of the same denomination; by "Letter," from one denomination to another.

RECORD OF MEMBERSHIP

Check Those No Longer Members	NAME	Date of Birth	RESIDENCE	RECEIVED HOW Confes-sion	Transfer	Letter	WHEN

NOTE—By "Transfer" is meant the change of membership, by proper authority, from one loc

RECORD OF MEMBERSHIP

RECEIVED BY WHOM	Date of Baptism	Date of Dedication by Parents	REMOVED Transfer	Letter	Expelled	Withdrawn	Died	WHEN	REMARKS (Where received, removed to what page, also what name if a woman and married since making of Record, cause of removal if expelled or withdrawn, etc.)

hurch to another of the same denomination; by "Letter," from one denomination to another.

RECORD OF MEMBERSHIP

Check Those No Longer Members	NAME	Date of Birth	RESIDENCE	RECEIVED			
				HOW			WHEN
				Confes-sion	Transfer	Letter	

NOTE—By "Transfer" is meant the change of membership, by proper authority, from one local

RECORD OF MEMBERSHIP

RECEIVED BY WHOM	Date of Baptism	Date of Dedication by Parents	REMOVED Transfer	Letter	Expelled	Withdrawn	Died	WHEN	REMARKS (Where received, removed to what page, also what name if a woman and married since making of Record, cause of removal if expelled or withdrawn, etc.)

urch to another of the same denomination; by "Letter," from one denomination to another.

RECORD OF MEMBERSHIP

Check Those No Longer Members	NAME	Date of Birth	RESIDENCE	RECEIVED			
				HOW			WHEN
				Confes-sion	Transfer	Letter	

NOTE—By "Transfer" is meant the change of membership, by proper authority, from one local

RECORD OF MEMBERSHIP

RECEIVED BY WHOM	Date of Baptism	Date of Dedication by Parents	REMOVED Transfer	Letter	Expelled	Withdrawn	Died	WHEN	REMARKS (Where received, removed to what page, also what name if a woman and married since making of Record, cause of removal if expelled or withdrawn, etc.)

hurch to another of the same denomination; by "Letter," from one denomination to another.

RECORD OF MEMBERSHIP

Check Those No Longer Members	NAME	Date of Birth	RESIDENCE	RECEIVED			
				HOW			WHEN
				Confes-sion	Transfer	Letter	

NOTE—By "Transfer" is meant the change of membership, by proper authority, from one local

RECORD OF MEMBERSHIP

RECEIVED BY WHOM	Date of Baptism	Date of Dedication by Parents	REMOVED Transfer	Letter	Expelled	Withdrawn	Died	WHEN	REMARKS (Where received, removed to what page, also what name if a woman and married since making of Record, cause of removal if expelled or withdrawn, etc.)

urch to another of the same denomination; by "Letter," from one denomination to another.

RECORD OF MEMBERSHIP

Check Those No Longer Members	NAME	Date of Birth	RESIDENCE	RECEIVED			
				HOW			WHEN
				Confes-sion	Transfer	Letter	

NOTE—By "Transfer" is meant the change of membership, by proper authority, from one loca

RECORD OF MEMBERSHIP

RECEIVED	Date of Baptism	Date of Dedication by Parents	REMOVED						REMARKS
BY WHOM			Transfer	Letter	Expelled	Withdrawn	Died	WHEN	(Where received, removed to what page, also what name if a woman and married since making of Record, cause of removal if expelled or withdrawn, etc.)

urch to another of the same denomination; by "Letter," from one denomination to another.

RECORD OF MEMBERSHIP

Check Those No Longer Members	NAME	Date of Birth	RESIDENCE	RECEIVED			
				HOW			WHEN
				Confes-sion	Transfer	Letter	

NOTE—By "Transfer" is meant the change of membership, by proper authority, from one loc

RECORD OF MEMBERSHIP

RECEIVED BY WHOM	Date of Baptism	Date of Dedication by Parents	REMOVED Transfer	Letter	Expelled	Withdrawn	Died	WHEN	REMARKS (Where received, removed to what page, also what name if a woman and married since making of Record, cause of removal if expelled or withdrawn, etc.)

'ch to another of the same denomination; by "Letter," from one denomination to another.

RECORD OF MEMBERSHIP

Check Those No Longer Members	NAME	Date of Birth	RESIDENCE	RECEIVED			
				HOW			WHEN
				Confes-sion	Transfer	Letter	

NOTE—By "Transfer" is meant the change of membership, by proper authority, from one lo

RECORD OF MEMBERSHIP

RECEIVED	Date of Baptism	Date of Dedication by Parents	REMOVED						REMARKS (Where received, removed to what page, also what name if a woman and married since making of Record, cause of removal if expelled or withdrawn, etc.)
BY WHOM			Transfer	Letter	Expelled	Withdrawn	Died	WHEN	

rch to another of the same denomination; by "Letter," from one denomination to another.

RECORD OF MEMBERSHIP

Check Those No Longer Members	NAME	Date of Birth	RESIDENCE	RECEIVED			
				HOW			WHEN
				Confes-sion	Transfer	Letter	

NOTE—By "Transfer" is meant the change of membership, by proper authority, from one loc

RECORD OF MEMBERSHIP

RECEIVED BY WHOM	Date of Baptism	Date of Dedication by Parents	REMOVED Transfer	Letter	Expelled	Withdrawn	Died	WHEN	REMARKS (Where received, removed to what page, also what name if a woman and married since making of Record, cause of removal if expelled or withdrawn, etc.)

urch to another of the same denomination; by "Letter," from one denomination to another.

RECORD OF MEMBERSHIP

Check Those No Longer Members	NAME	Date of Birth	RESIDENCE	RECEIVED			
				HOW			WHEN
				Confes-sion	Transfer	Letter	

NOTE—By "Transfer" is meant the change of membership, by proper authority, from one loca

RECORD OF MEMBERSHIP

RECEIVED BY WHOM	Date of Baptism	Date of Dedication by Parents	REMOVED Transfer	Letter	Expelled	Withdrawn	Died	WHEN	REMARKS (Where received, removed to what page, also what name if a woman and married since making of Record, cause of removal if expelled or withdrawn, etc.)

urch to another of the same denomination; by "Letter," from one denomination to another.

RECORD OF MEMBERSHIP

Check Those No Longer Members	NAME	Date of Birth	RESIDENCE	RECEIVED			
				HOW			WHEN
				Confes-sion	Transfer	Letter	

NOTE—By "Transfer" is meant the change of membership, by proper authority, from one local

RECORD OF MEMBERSHIP

RECEIVED	Date of Baptism	Date of Dedication by Parents	REMOVED						REMARKS (Where received, removed to what page, also what name if a woman and married since making of Record, cause of removal if expelled or withdrawn, etc.)
BY WHOM			Transfer	Letter	Expelled	Withdrawn	Died	WHEN	

hurch to another of the same denomination; by "Letter," from one denomination to another.

RECORD OF MEMBERSHIP

Check Those No Longer	NAME	Date of Birth	RESIDENCE	RECEIVED			
				HOW			WHEN
				Confes-sion	Transfer	Letter	

NOTE—By "Transfer" is meant the change of membership, by proper authority, from one local

RECORD OF MEMBERSHIP

RECEIVED BY WHOM	Date of Baptism	Date of Dedication by Parents	REMOVED Transfer	Letter	Expelled	Withdrawn	Died	WHEN	REMARKS (Where received, removed to what page, also what name if a woman and married since making of Record, cause of removal if expelled or withdrawn, etc.)

:hurch to another of the same denomination; by "Letter," from one denomination to another.

RECORD OF MEMBERSHIP

Check Those No Longer Members	NAME	Date of Birth	RESIDENCE	RECEIVED HOW Confes-sion	Transfer	Letter	WHEN

NOTE—By "Transfer" is meant the change of membership, by proper authority, from one local

RECORD OF MEMBERSHIP

RECEIVED BY WHOM	Date of Baptism	Date of Dedication by Parents	REMOVED Transfer	Letter	Expelled	Withdrawn	Died	WHEN	REMARKS (Where received, removed to what page, also what name if a woman and married since making of Record, cause of removal if expelled or withdrawn, etc.)

urch to another of the same denomination; by "Letter," from one denomination to another.

RECORD OF MEMBERSHIP

Check Those No Longer Members	NAME	Date of Birth	RESIDENCE	RECEIVED			
				HOW			WHEN
				Confes-sion	Transfer	Letter	

NOTE—By "Transfer" is meant the change of membership, by proper authority, from one loc

RECORD OF MEMBERSHIP

RECEIVED BY WHOM	Date of Baptism	Date of Dedication by Parents	REMOVED Transfer	Letter	Expelled	Withdrawn	Died	WHEN	REMARKS (Where received, removed to what page, also what name if a woman and married since making of Record, cause of removal if expelled or withdrawn, etc.)

:h to another of the same denomination; by "Letter," from one denomination to another.

RECORD OF MEMBERSHIP

Check Those No Longer Members	NAME	Date of Birth	RESIDENCE	RECEIVED			
				HOW			WHE
				Confes-sion	Transfer	Letter	

NOTE—By "Transfer" is meant the change of membership, by proper authority, from one l

RECORD OF MEMBERSHIP

RECEIVED BY WHOM	Date of Baptism	Date of Dedication by Parents	REMOVED Transfer	Letter	Expelled	Withdrawn	Died	WHEN	REMARKS (Where received, removed to what page, also what name if a woman and married since making of Record, cause of removal if expelled or withdrawn, etc.)

rch to another of the same denomination; by "Letter," from one denomination to another.

RECORD OF MEMBERSHIP

Check Those No Longer Members	NAME	Date of Birth	RESIDENCE	RECEIVED			
				HOW			WHEN
				Confes-sion	Transfer	Letter	

NOTE—By "Transfer" is meant the change of membership, by proper authority, from one lo

RECORD OF MEMBERSHIP

RECEIVED BY WHOM	Date of Baptism	Date of Dedication by Parents	REMOVED Transfer	Letter	Expelled	Withdrawn	Died	WHEN	REMARKS (Where received, removed to what page, also what name if a woman and married since making of Record, cause of removal if expelled or withdrawn, etc.)

urch to another of the same denomination; by "Letter," from one denomination to another.

RECORD OF MEMBERSHIP

Check Those No Longer Members	NAME	Date of Birth	RESIDENCE	RECEIVED			
				HOW			WHEN
				Confes-sion	Transfer	Letter	

NOTE—By "Transfer" is meant the change of membership, by proper authority, from one loca

RECORD OF MEMBERSHIP

RECEIVED BY WHOM	Date of Baptism	Date of Dedication by Parents	REMOVED Transfer	Letter	Expelled	Withdrawn	Died	WHEN	REMARKS (Where received, removed to what page, also what name if a woman and married since making of Record, cause of removal if expelled or withdrawn, etc.)

urch to another of the same denomination; by "Letter," from one denomination to another.

RECORD OF MEMBERSHIP

Check Those No Longer Members	NAME	Date of Birth	RESIDENCE	RECEIVED			
				HOW			WHEN
				Confes-sion	Transfer	Letter	

NOTE—By "Transfer" is meant the change of membership, by proper authority, from one loca

RECORD OF MEMBERSHIP

RECEIVED BY WHOM	Date of Baptism	Date of Dedication by Parents	REMOVED Transfer	Letter	Expelled	Withdrawn	Died	WHEN	REMARKS (Where received, removed to what page, also what name if a woman and married since making of Record, cause of removal if expelled or withdrawn, etc.)

urch to another of the same denomination; by "Letter," from one denomination to another.

RECORD OF MEMBERSHIP

Check Those No Longer Members	NAME	Date of Birth	RESIDENCE	RECEIVED			
				HOW			WHEN
				Confes-sion	Transfer	Letter	

NOTE—By "Transfer" is meant the change of membership, by proper authority, from one loca

RECORD OF MEMBERSHIP

RECEIVED			REMOVED						REMARKS
BY WHOM	Date of Baptism	Date of Dedication by Parents	Transfer	Letter	Expelled	Withdrawn	Died	WHEN	(Where received, removed to what page, also what name if a woman and married since making of Record, cause of removal if expelled or withdrawn, etc.)

urch to another of the same denomination; by "Letter," from one denomination to another.

O

RECORD OF MEMBERSHIP

Check Those No Longer Members	NAME	Date of Birth	RESIDENCE	RECEIVED			
				HOW			WHEN
				Confes-sion	Transfer	Letter	

NOTE—By "Transfer" is meant the change of membership, by proper authority, from one loca

RECORD OF MEMBERSHIP

RECEIVED			REMOVED						REMARKS
BY WHOM	Date of Baptism	Date of Dedication by Parents	Transfer	Letter	Expelled	Withdrawn	Died	WHEN	(Where received, removed to what page, also what name if a woman and married since making of Record, cause of removal if expelled or withdrawn, etc.)

hurch to another of the same denomination; by "Letter," from one denomination to another.

RECORD OF MEMBERSHIP

Check Those No Longer Members	NAME	Date of Birth	RESIDENCE	RECEIVED			
				HOW			WHEN
				Confes-sion	Transfer	Letter	

NOTE—By "Transfer" is meant the change of membership, by proper authority, from one local

RECORD OF MEMBERSHIP

RECEIVED BY WHOM	Date of Baptism	Date of Dedication by Parents	REMOVED Transfer	Letter	Expelled	Withdrawn	Died	WHEN	REMARKS (Where received, removed to what page, also what name if a woman and married since making of Record, cause of removal if expelled or withdrawn, etc.)

church to another of the same denomination; by "Letter," from one denomination to another.

RECORD OF MEMBERSHIP

Check Those No Longer Members	NAME	Date of Birth	RESIDENCE	RECEIVED			
				HOW			WHEN
				Confes-sion	Transfer	Letter	

NOTE—By "Transfer" is meant the change of membership, by proper authority, from one local

RECORD OF MEMBERSHIP

RECEIVED BY WHOM	Date of Baptism	Date of Dedication by Parents	REMOVED Transfer	Letter	Expelled	Withdrawn	Died	WHEN	REMARKS (Where received, removed to what page, also what name if a woman and married since making of Record, cause of removal if expelled or withdrawn, etc.)

…rch to another of the same denomination; by "Letter," from one denomination to another.

RECORD OF MEMBERSHIP

Check Those No Longer Members	NAME	Date of Birth	RESIDENCE	RECEIVED			
				HOW			WHEN
				Confes-sion	Transfer	Letter	

NOTE—By "Transfer" is meant the change of membership, by proper authority, from one loc

RECORD OF MEMBERSHIP

RECEIVED BY WHOM	Date of Baptism	Date of Dedication by Parents	REMOVED Transfer	Letter	Expelled	Withdrawn	Died	WHEN	REMARKS (Where received, removed to what page, also what name if a woman and married since making of Record, cause of removal if expelled or withdrawn, etc.)

urch to another of the same denomination; by "Letter," from one denomination to another.

RECORD OF MEMBERSHIP

Check Those No Longer Members	NAME	Date of Birth	RESIDENCE	RECEIVED			
				HOW			WHEN
				Confes-sion	Transfer	Letter	

NOTE—By "Transfer" is meant the change of membership, by proper authority, from one loc

RECORD OF MEMBERSHIP

RECEIVED BY WHOM	Date of Baptism	Date of Dedication by Parents	REMOVED Transfer	Letter	Expelled	Withdrawn	Died	WHEN	REMARKS (Where received, removed to what page, also what name if a woman and married since making of Record, cause of removal if expelled or withdrawn, etc.)

rch to another of the same denomination; by "Letter," from one denomination to another.

RECORD OF MEMBERSHIP

Check Those No Longer Members	NAME	Date of Birth	RESIDENCE	RECEIVED: HOW: Confes-sion	RECEIVED: HOW: Transfer	RECEIVED: HOW: Letter	RECEIVED: WHEN

NOTE—By "Transfer" is meant the change of membership, by proper authority, from one loca

RECORD OF MEMBERSHIP

RECEIVED	Date of Baptism	Date of Dedication by Parents	REMOVED						REMARKS (Where received, removed to what page, also what name if a woman and married since making of Record, cause of removal if expelled or withdrawn, etc.)
BY WHOM			Transfer	Letter	Expelled	Withdrawn	Died	WHEN	

urch to another of the same denomination; by "Letter," from one denomination to another.

RECORD OF MEMBERSHIP

Check Those No Longer Members	NAME	Date of Birth	RESIDENCE	RECEIVED			
				HOW			WHEN
				Confes-sion	Transfer	Letter	

NOTE—By "Transfer" is meant the change of membership, by proper authority, from one loca

RECORD OF MEMBERSHIP

RECEIVED	Date of Baptism	Date of Dedication by Parents	REMOVED						REMARKS (Where received, removed to what page, also what name if a woman and married since making of Record, cause of removal if expelled or withdrawn, etc.)
BY WHOM			Transfer	Letter	Expelled	Withdrawn	Died	WHEN	

urch to another of the same denomination; by "Letter," from one denomination to another.

RECORD OF MEMBERSHIP

Check Those No Longer Members	NAME	Date of Birth	RESIDENCE	RECEIVED			
				HOW			WHEN
				Confes-sion	Transfer	Letter	

NOTE—By "Transfer" is meant the change of membership, by proper authority, from one loca

RECORD OF MEMBERSHIP

RECEIVED BY WHOM	Date of Baptism	Date of Dedication by Parents	REMOVED Transfer	Letter	Expelled	Withdrawn	Died	WHEN	REMARKS (Where received, removed to what page, also what name if a woman and married since making of Record, cause of removal if expelled or withdrawn, etc.)

urch to another of the same denomination; by "Letter," from one denomination to another.

RECORD OF MEMBERSHIP

Check Those No Longer Members	NAME	Date of Birth	RESIDENCE	RECEIVED			
				HOW			WHEN
				Confes-sion	Transfer	Letter	

NOTE—By "Transfer" is meant the change of membership, by proper authority, from one local

RECORD OF MEMBERSHIP

RECEIVED BY WHOM	Date of Baptism	Date of Dedication by Parents	REMOVED Transfer	Letter	Expelled	Withdrawn	Died	WHEN	REMARKS (Where received, removed to what page, also what name if a woman and married since making of Record, cause of removal if expelled or withdrawn, etc.)

urch to another of the same denomination; by "Letter," from one denomination to another.

RECORD OF MEMBERSHIP

Check Those No Longer Members	NAME	Date of Birth	RESIDENCE	RECEIVED			
				HOW			WHEN
				Confes-sion	Transfer	Letter	

NOTE—By "Transfer" is meant the change of membership, by proper authority, from one loca

RECORD OF MEMBERSHIP

RECEIVED BY WHOM	Date of Baptism	Date of Dedication by Parents	REMOVED Transfer	Letter	Expelled	Withdrawn	Died	WHEN	REMARKS (Where received, removed to what page, also what name if a woman and married since making of Record, cause of removal if expelled or withdrawn, etc.)

urch to another of the same denomination; by "Letter," from one denomination to another.

RECORD OF MEMBERSHIP

Check Those No Longer Members	NAME	Date of Birth	RESIDENCE	RECEIVED			
				HOW			WHEN
				Confes-sion	Transfer	Letter	

NOTE—By "Transfer" is meant the change of membership, by proper authority, from one loc

RECORD OF MEMBERSHIP

RECEIVED	Date of Baptism	Date of Dedication by Parents	REMOVED						REMARKS (Where received, removed to what page, also what name if a woman and married since making of Record, cause of removal if expelled or withdrawn, etc.)
BY WHOM			Transfer	Letter	Expelled	Withdrawn	Died	WHEN	

rch to another of the same denomination; by "Letter," from one denomination to another.

RECORD OF MEMBERSHIP

Check Those No Longer Members	NAME	Date of Birth	RESIDENCE	RECEIVED HOW Confes-sion	Transfer	Letter	WHEN

NOTE—By "Transfer" is meant the change of membership, by proper authority, from one loc

RECORD OF MEMBERSHIP

RECEIVED BY WHOM	Date of Baptism	Date of Dedication by Parents	REMOVED Transfer	Letter	Expelled	Withdrawn	Died	WHEN	REMARKS (Where received, removed to what page, also what name if a woman and married since making of Record, cause of removal if expelled or withdrawn, etc.)

ch to another of the same denomination; by "Letter," from one denomination to another.

RECORD OF MEMBERSHIP

Check Those No Longer Members	NAME	Date of Birth	RESIDENCE	RECEIVED			
				HOW			WHE
				Confes-sion	Transfer	Letter	

NOTE—By "Transfer" is meant the change of membership, by proper authority, from one lo

RECORD OF MEMBERSHIP

RECEIVED BY WHOM	Date of Baptism	Date of Dedication by Parents	REMOVED Transfer	REMOVED Letter	REMOVED Expelled	REMOVED Withdrawn	REMOVED Died	REMOVED WHEN	REMARKS (Where received, removed to what page, also what name if a woman and married since making of Record, cause of removal if expelled or withdrawn, etc.)

'ch to another of the same denomination; by "Letter," from one denomination to another.

RECORD OF MEMBERSHIP

Check Those No Longer Members	NAME	Date of Birth	RESIDENCE	RECEIVED			
				HOW			WHEN
				Confes-sion	Transfer	Letter	

NOTE—By "Transfer" is meant the change of membership, by proper authority, from one loc

RECORD OF MEMBERSHIP

RECEIVED			REMOVED						REMARKS
BY WHOM	Date of Baptism	Date of Dedication by Parents	Transfer	Letter	Expelled	Withdrawn	Died	WHEN	(Where received, removed to what page, also what name if a woman and married since making of Record, cause of removal if expelled or withdrawn, etc.)

rch to another of the same denomination; by "Letter," from one denomination to another.

RECORD OF MEMBERSHIP

Check Those No Longer Members	NAME	Date of Birth	RESIDENCE	RECEIVED — HOW: Confes-sion	RECEIVED — HOW: Transfer	RECEIVED — HOW: Letter	RECEIVED — WHEN

NOTE—By "Transfer" is meant the change of membership, by proper authority, from one loca

RECORD OF MEMBERSHIP

RECEIVED	Date of Baptism	Date of Dedication by Parents	REMOVED						REMARKS (Where received, removed to what page, also what name if a woman and married since making of Record, cause of removal if expelled or withdrawn, etc.)
BY WHOM			Transfer	Letter	Expelled	Withdrawn	Died	WHEN	

urch to another of the same denomination; by "Letter," from one denomination to another.

RECORD OF MEMBERSHIP

Check Those No Longer Members	NAME	Date of Birth	RESIDENCE	RECEIVED			
				HOW			WHEN
				Confes-sion	Transfer	Letter	

NOTE—By "Transfer" is meant the change of membership, by proper authority, from one local

RECORD OF MEMBERSHIP

RECEIVED BY WHOM	Date of Baptism	Date of Dedication by Parents	REMOVED Transfer	Letter	Expelled	Withdrawn	Died	WHEN	REMARKS (Where received, removed to what page, also what name if a woman and married since making of Record, cause of removal if expelled or withdrawn, etc.)

hurch to another of the same denomination; by "Letter," from one denomination to another.

RECORD OF MEMBERSHIP

Check Those No Longer Members	NAME	Date of Birth	RESIDENCE	RECEIVED HOW: Confes-sion	RECEIVED HOW: Transfer	RECEIVED HOW: Letter	RECEIVED WHEN

NOTE—By "Transfer" is meant the change of membership, by proper authority, from one local

RECORD OF MEMBERSHIP

RECEIVED BY WHOM	Date of Baptism	Date of Dedication by Parents	REMOVED Transfer	Letter	Expelled	Withdrawn	Died	WHEN	REMARKS (Where received, removed to what page, also what name if a woman and married since making of Record, cause of removal if expelled or withdrawn, etc.)

hurch to another of the same denomination; by "Letter," from one denomination to another.

RECORD OF MEMBERSHIP

Check Those No Longer Members	NAME	Date of Birth	RESIDENCE	RECEIVED			
				HOW			WHEN
				Confes-sion	Transfer	Letter	

NOTE—By "Transfer" is meant the change of membership, by proper authority, from one local

RECORD OF MEMBERSHIP

RECEIVED			REMOVED						REMARKS (Where received, removed to what page, also what name if a woman and married since making of Record, cause of removal if expelled or withdrawn, etc.)
BY WHOM	Date of Baptism	Date of Dedication by Parents	Transfer	Letter	Expelled	Withdrawn	Died	WHEN	

urch to another of the same denomination; by "Letter," from one denomination to another.

RECORD OF MEMBERSHIP

Check Those No Longer Members	NAME	Date of Birth	RESIDENCE	RECEIVED			
				HOW			WHEN
				Confes-sion	Transfer	Letter	

NOTE—By "Transfer" is meant the change of membership, by proper authority, from one loca

RECORD OF MEMBERSHIP

RECEIVED	Date of Baptism	Date of Dedication by Parents	REMOVED						REMARKS (Where received, removed to what page, also what name if a woman and married since making of Record, cause of removal if expelled or withdrawn, etc.)
BY WHOM			Transfer	Letter	Expelled	Withdrawn	Died	WHEN	

urch to another of the same denomination; by "Letter," from one denomination to another.

RECORD OF MEMBERSHIP

Check Those No Longer Members	NAME	Date of Birth	RESIDENCE	RECEIVED			
				HOW			WHEN
				Confes-sion	Transfer	Letter	

NOTE—By "Transfer" is meant the change of membership, by proper authority, from one loc

RECORD OF MEMBERSHIP

RECEIVED	Date of Baptism	Date of Dedication by Parents	REMOVED						REMARKS (Where received, removed to what page, also what name if a woman and married since making of Record, cause of removal if expelled or withdrawn, etc.)
BY WHOM			Transfer	Letter	Expelled	Withdrawn	Died	WHEN	

rch to another of the same denomination; by "Letter," from one denomination to another.

RECORD OF MEMBERSHIP

Check Those No Longer Members	NAME	Date of Birth	RESIDENCE	RECEIVED			
				HOW			WHEN
				Confes-sion	Transfer	Letter	

NOTE—By "Transfer" is meant the change of membership, by proper authority, from one loc

RECORD OF MEMBERSHIP

RECEIVED			REMOVED						REMARKS
BY WHOM	Date of Baptism	Date of Dedication by Parents	Transfer	Letter	Expelled	Withdrawn	Died	WHEN	(Where received, removed to what page, also what name if a woman and married since making of Record, cause of removal if expelled or withdrawn, etc.)

rch to another of the same denomination; by "Letter," from one denomination to another.

RECORD OF MEMBERSHIP

Check Those No Longer Members	NAME	Date of Birth	RESIDENCE	RECEIVED			
				HOW			WHEN
				Confes-sion	Transfer	Letter	

NOTE—By "Transfer" is meant the change of membership, by proper authority, from one loc

RECORD OF MEMBERSHIP

RECEIVED	Date of Baptism	Date of Dedication by Parents	REMOVED						REMARKS (Where received, removed to what page, also what name if a woman and married since making of Record, cause of removal if expelled or withdrawn, etc.)
BY WHOM			Transfer	Letter	Expelled	Withdrawn	Died	WHEN	

rch to another of the same denomination; by "Letter," from one denomination to another.

RECORD OF MEMBERSHIP

Check Those No Longer Members	NAME	Date of Birth	RESIDENCE	RECEIVED			
				HOW			WHEN
				Confes-sion	Transfer	Letter	

NOTE—By "Transfer" is meant the change of membership, by proper authority, from one loc

RECORD OF MEMBERSHIP

RECEIVED BY WHOM	Date of Baptism	Date of Dedication by Parents	REMOVED Transfer	Letter	Expelled	Withdrawn	Died	WHEN	REMARKS (Where received, removed to what page, also what name if a woman and married since making of Record, cause of removal if expelled or withdrawn, etc.)

hurch to another of the same denomination; by "Letter," from one denomination to another.

RECORD OF CHILDREN BORN

CHILD'S NAME		FATHER'S NAME	A Member?	MOTHER'S MAIDEN NAME	Member?
Surname	Christian Name				

NOTE—Mark "Father's" and "Mother's" names with an (X) if members of church.

RECORD OF CHILDREN DEDICATED

PLACE OF BIRTH	Date of Birth	PLACE OF DEDICATION	Date of Dedication	Certificate Given	OFFICIATING MINISTER

NOTE—Indicate Certificates given with an (X).

RECORD OF CHILDREN BORN

CHILD'S NAME		FATHER'S NAME	A Member?	MOTHER'S MAIDEN NAME	Member?
Surname	Christian Name				

NOTE—Mark "Father's" and "Mother's" names with an (X) if members of church.

RECORD OF CHILDREN DEDICATED

PLACE OF BIRTH	Date of Birth	PLACE OF DEDICATION	Date of Dedication	Certificate Given	OFFICIATING MINISTER

NOTE—Indicate Certificates given with an (X).

RECORD OF CHILDREN BORN

CHILD'S NAME		FATHER'S NAME	A Member?	MOTHER'S MAIDEN NAME
Surname	Christian Name			

NOTE—Mark "Father's" and "Mother's" names with an (X) if members of church.

RECORD OF CHILDREN DEDICATED

PLACE OF BIRTH	Date of Birth	PLACE OF DEDICATION	Date of Dedication	Certificate Given	OFFICIATING MINISTER

NOTE—Indicate Certificates given with an (X).

RECORD OF CHILDREN BORN

CHILD'S NAME		FATHER'S NAME	A Member?	MOTHER'S MAIDEN NAME
Surname	Christian Name			

NOTE—Mark "Father's" and "Mother's" names with an (X) if members of church.

RECORD OF CHILDREN DEDICATED

PLACE OF BIRTH	Date of Birth	PLACE OF DEDICATION	Date of Dedication	Certificate Given	OFFICIATING MINISTER

NOTE—Indicate Certificates given with an (X).

RECORD OF CHILDREN BORN

CHILD'S NAME		FATHER'S NAME	A Member?	MOTHER'S MAIDEN NAME
Surname	Christian Name			

NOTE—Mark "Father's" and "Mother's" names with an (X) if members of church.

RECORD OF CHILDREN DEDICATED

PLACE OF BIRTH	Date of Birth	PLACE OF DEDICATION	Date of Dedication	Certificate Given	OFFICIATING MINISTER

NOTE—Indicate Certificates given with an (X).

RECORD OF CHILDREN BORN

CHILD'S NAME		FATHER'S NAME	A Member?	MOTHER'S MAIDEN NAME
Surname	Christian Name			

NOTE—Mark "Father's" and "Mother's" names with an (X) if members of church.

RECORD OF CHILDREN DEDICATED

PLACE OF BIRTH	Date of Birth	PLACE OF DEDICATION	Date of Dedication	Certificate Given	OFFICIATING MINISTER

NOTE—Indicate Certificates given with an (X).

RECORD OF CHILDREN BORN

CHILD'S NAME		FATHER'S NAME	A Member?	MOTHER'S MAIDEN NAME
Surname	Christian Name			

NOTE—Mark "Father's" and "Mother's" names with an (X) if members of church.

RECORD OF CHILDREN DEDICATED

PLACE OF BIRTH	Date of Birth	PLACE OF DEDICATION	Date of Dedication	Certificate Given	OFFICIATING MINISTER

NOTE—Indicate Certificates given with an (X).

RECORD OF CHILDREN BORN

CHILD'S NAME		FATHER'S NAME	A Member?	MOTHER'S MAIDEN NAME
Surname	Christian Name			

NOTE—Mark "Father's" and "Mother's" names with an (X) if members of church.

RECORD OF CHILDREN DEDICATED

PLACE OF BIRTH	Date of Birth	PLACE OF DEDICATION	Date of Dedication	Certificate Given	OFFICIATING MINISTER

NOTE—Indicate Certificates given with an (X).

RECORD OF CHILDREN BORN

CHILD'S NAME		FATHER'S NAME	A Member?	MOTHER'S MAIDEN NAME	A Member?
Surname	Christian Name				

NOTE—Mark "Father's" and "Mother's" names with an (X) if members of church.

RECORD OF CHILDREN DEDICATED

PLACE OF BIRTH	Date of Birth	PLACE OF DEDICATION	Date of Dedication	Certificate Given	OFFICIATING MINISTER

NOTE—Indicate Certificates given with an (X).

RECORD OF CHILDREN BORN

CHILD'S NAME		FATHER'S NAME	A Member?	MOTHER'S MAIDEN NAME	Member?
Surname	Christian Name				

NOTE—Mark "Father's" and "Mother's" names with an (X) if members of church.

RECORD OF CHILDREN DEDICATED

PLACE OF BIRTH	Date of Birth	PLACE OF DEDICATION	Date of Dedication	Certificate Given	OFFICIATING MINISTER

NOTE—Indicate Certificates given with an (X).

RECORD OF CHILDREN BORN

CHILD'S NAME		FATHER'S NAME	A Member?	MOTHER'S MAIDEN NAME	Member?
Surname	Christian Name				

NOTE—Mark "Father's" and "Mother's" names with an (X) if members of church.

RECORD OF CHILDREN DEDICATED

PLACE OF BIRTH	Date of Birth	PLACE OF DEDICATION	Date of Dedication	Certificate Given	OFFICIATING MINISTER

NOTE—Indicate Certificates given with an (X).

RECORD OF CHILDREN BORN

CHILD'S NAME		FATHER'S NAME	A Member?	MOTHER'S MAIDEN NAME	Member?
Surname	Christian Name				

NOTE—Mark "Father's" and "Mother's" names with an (X) if members of church.

RECORD OF CHILDREN DEDICATED

PLACE OF BIRTH	Date of Birth	PLACE OF DEDICATION	Date of Dedication	Certificate Given	OFFICIATING MINISTER

NOTE—Indicate Certificates given with an (X).

RECORD OF CHILDREN BORN

CHILD'S NAME		FATHER'S NAME	A Member?	MOTHER'S MAIDEN NAME
Surname	Christian Name			

NOTE—Mark "Father's" and "Mother's" names with an (X) if members of church.

RECORD OF CHILDREN DEDICATED

PLACE OF BIRTH	Date of Birth	PLACE OF DEDICATION	Date of Dedication	Certificate Given	OFFICIATING MINISTER

NOTE—Indicate Certificates given with an (X).

RECORD OF CHILDREN BORN

CHILD'S NAME		FATHER'S NAME	A Member?	MOTHER'S MAIDEN NAME	Member?
Surname	Christian Name				

NOTE—Mark "Father's" and "Mother's" names with an (X) if members of church.

RECORD OF CHILDREN DEDICATED

PLACE OF BIRTH	Date of Birth	PLACE OF DEDICATION	Date of Dedication	Certificate Given	OFFICIATING MINISTER

NOTE—Indicate Certificates given with an (X).

RECORD OF CHILDREN BORN

CHILD'S NAME		FATHER'S NAME	A Member?	MOTHER'S MAIDEN NAME	Member?
Surname	Christian Name				

NOTE—Mark "Father's" and "Mother's" names with an (X) if members of church.

RECORD OF CHILDREN DEDICATED

PLACE OF BIRTH	Date of Birth	PLACE OF DEDICATION	Date of Dedication	Certificate Given	OFFICIATING MINISTER

NOTE—Indicate Certificates given with an (X).

RECORD OF CHILDREN BORN

CHILD'S NAME		FATHER'S NAME	A Member?	MOTHER'S MAIDEN NAME	Member?
Surname	Christian Name				

NOTE—Mark "Father's" and "Mother's" names with an (X) if members of church.

RECORD OF CHILDREN DEDICATED

PLACE OF BIRTH	Date of Birth	PLACE OF DEDICATION	Date of Dedication	Certificate Given	OFFICIATING MINISTER

NOTE—Indicate Certificates given with an (X).

RECORD OF CHILDREN BORN

CHILD'S NAME		FATHER'S NAME	A Member?	MOTHER'S MAIDEN NAME	Member?
Surname	Christian Name				

NOTE—Mark "Father's" and "Mother's" names with an (X) if members of church.

RECORD OF CHILDREN DEDICATED

PLACE OF BIRTH	Date of Birth	PLACE OF DEDICATION	Date of Dedication	Certificate Given	OFFICIATING MINISTER

NOTE—Indicate Certificates given with an (X).

RECORD OF CHILDREN BORN

CHILD'S NAME		FATHER'S NAME	A Member?	MOTHER'S MAIDEN NAME	Member?
Surname	Christian Name				

NOTE—Mark "Father's" and "Mother's" names with an (X) if members of church.

RECORD OF CHILDREN DEDICATED

PLACE OF BIRTH	Date of Birth	PLACE OF DEDICATION	Date of Dedication	Certificate Given	OFFICIATING MINISTER

NOTE—Indicate Certificates given with an (X).

MARRIAGES

NAME	Age	When	Where	By Whom
His	His		City or Country	
Her	Her		State	Witness

MARRIAGES

NAME	Age	When	Where	By Whom
His	His		City or Country	
Her	Her		State	Witness

MARRIAGES

NAME	Age	When	Where	By Whom
His	His		City or Country	
Her	Her		State	Witness

MARRIAGES

NAME	Age	When	Where	By Whom
His	His		City or Country	
Her	Her		State	Witness

MARRIAGES

NAME	Age	When	Where	By Whom
His	His		City or Country	
Her	Her		State	Witness

MARRIAGES

NAME	Age	When	Where	By Whom
His	His		City or Country	
Her	Her		State	Witness

MARRIAGES

NAME	Age	When	Where	By Whom
His	His		City or Country	
Her	Her		State	Witness

MARRIAGES

NAME	Age	When	Where	By Whom
His	His		City or Country	
Her	Her		State	Witness

MARRIAGES

NAME	Age	When	Where	By Whom
His	His		City or Country	
Her	Her		State	Witness

MARRIAGES

NAME	Age	When	Where	By Whom
His	His		City or Country	
Her	Her		State	Witness

MARRIAGES

NAME	Age	When	Where	By Whom
His	His		City or Country	
Her	Her		State	Witness

MARRIAGES

NAME	Age	When	Where	By Whom
His	His		City or Country	
Her	Her		State	Witness

OTHER RECORDS